"I know what
    my feelings are,
    But...
I don't know what
    I'm feeling."

My thoughts,
your thoughts,
deep thoughts

SHERMAN DICKINSON

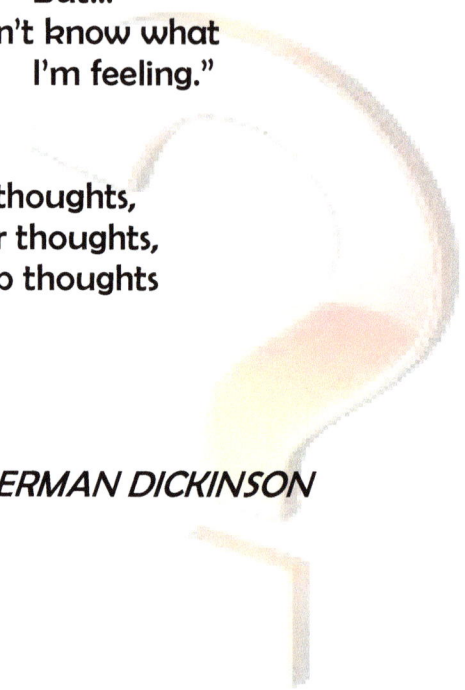

Dedicated to:

God the Father,
Mother, Ollie Konickey,
Father, James Konickey,
First born, Amber,
Jr., Little Sherman,
Brother, James Fitzgerald,
Sister, Janice.
Because of each of you,
I am what I am, and who I am today.

Sorry, I had to tell *somebody!*

HIS IS GOOD READING!

Poetry which takes you on a journey. Inside is found descriptions of very good experiences ,also revealed are struggles with uncertain outcomes. Some are stories know ,some known of. There is a need to stay centered, confident of the destination.

"...I then got another revelation of the need to press on in the face of difficulty keeping your eye on the goal. The road was not without obstacles; rocks, gravel, little gullies, lots of uneven spots, sometime having to go sideways a bit to get to a spot where I could continue to go up (another revelation). May I take this pause to interject ; I began to relish the value of this undertaking more than I could have hoped."
...Excerpt from the introduction.

Relaxing prose causing the spirit to renew its zeal.
The beauty of reading is control over the paced of the story.

LET US TAKE A JOURNEY!

THIS VISIT

Thank You Lord.
Thank You for what I think
I feel I'm feeling.
Thank You for putting
A part inside
I don't control,
Which allows me contact
With you.
Thank You Lord
For confusions past.
It showed me
Your hand.
Thank You for the moments
I can't explain.
It makes me BELIEVE
You are real.
I know the struggle
Is with me.
Thank You Lord,
For Your hand through this.
Thank You for the growth.
Thank You for the protection,
And the times
You let me see You work.
Small things,
But real things.
Thank You for now Lord.
I have really enjoyed
This visit.

Preface

I praise God for giving me the ability to write My Thoughts and experiences. My prayer is, you will find some of Your Thoughts in the pages to follow. We go through life's events finding challenges, as well as, blessings. We find surprises also. We constantly amaze ourselves at our capacity to do things when called upon. We are often an encouragement to others by way of our Deep Thoughts. God blesses us to have them for ourselves, as well as, to share them with others. My desire is to take you on a journey through some of my pains, my joys, my hopes, my prayers. When all is said and done, we have peace in knowing God is a good God and we can see Him work in so many people we meet. I pray to be one of those people and I pray you will be one of those people as well.

I continue to give honor to God for bringing me through so much of what I have gotten myself into. Allowing me to work in my church has afforded me more blessings than I could have ever imagined. The aforementioned being true, I wonder why I struggle with what God may want to make of me. I can only say, much of the joy you will feel will not manifest itself until after you have been willing to be used.

Many thanks to you Mom, for birthing me and showing me sound doctrine. Many thanks to you Dad, for being the only father I've ever known, thank-you also for teaching me responsibility, which I'm still trying to handle. Thank You Lord, for my children and the times they have given me. Thank You for the people You've blessed me to meet, as You used them to show me answers hidden. Thank You most of all, for the covering and allowing me to be an instrument sometimes.

"...While I sat there looking around enjoying the feeling of accomplishment, I saw two people coming up the trail and they took the best road, were making good time and began to struggle. The thought came to me, "you may be moved to go down to help them but you had to struggle from there to get where you are now. You can tell them how to help themselves by encouraging them to come where you are". I did. They turned around at about half way, just before the easy part came. On my way down, I noticed how fast one began to go down after struggling so hard to get to an elevated place. Had I wanted to turn around, the downhill pull would require twice the effort to stop than to continue down! This is a revelation indeed!"

... From the introduction.

TABLE OF CONTENTS
INTRODUCTION

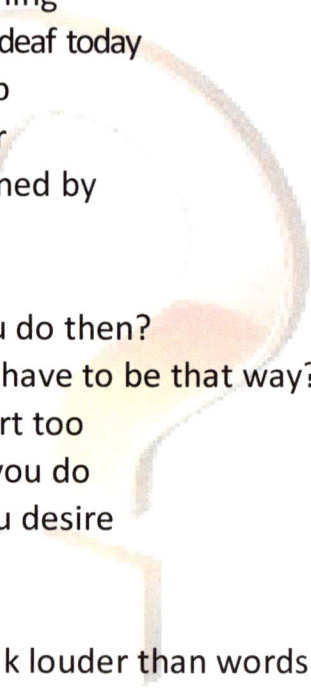

- It's okay to be scared
- Death is no stranger
- Because of
- Emotional treasures
- Artist
- Time passes so quickly
- Your Parent
- Been there all the time
- You were made for me
- Truly a gift
- Your face
- On so many levels
- It still works
- No matter what
- This visit
- How do you feel?
- Nothing to lose
- The prize
- You seek it
- Things I call relaxing
- Wasting time?
- We don't believe it
- Have you ever wondered?
- Looking for one
- I will celebrate differently
- Right now
- Why?
- I want to be in love
- Open our eyes
- I want to be a witness

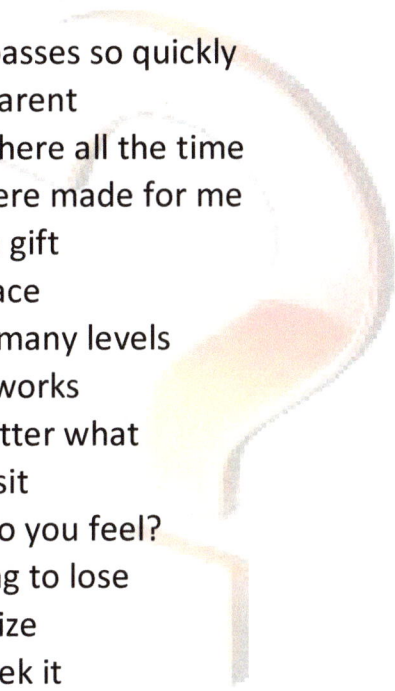

- So you're in love?
- Mystery of emotions
- Why children?
- What can you do?
- God is waiting
- Before
- That is where the insides start
- In spite of all the light
- I know what my feelings are
- A mate, a lover, a friend

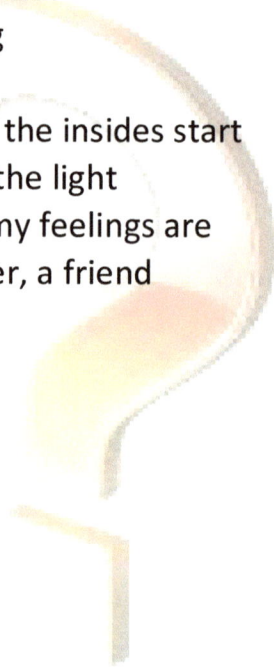

Introduction

A Word from the Mountaintop! To be blessed with a desire to get closer to God in any way possible is joyous in itself. For sure, we get glimpses of His hand in all that we do daily if we are paying attention. There is a retreat in Riverside, which has a cross atop a hill requiring a rather steep climb to reach. I got the urge to make the trek, while attending a retreat there: On my way up to the cross I ran into a man of God, his name was Jeremiah; I asked him the way to the cross at the top of the hill. Jeremiah, with a big smile, welcomed me and began to tell me the way. "Well", he began "there are coyote up there but they probably won't bother you". My reply," if they get after me they will be too tired by the time they catch up." This was my first revelation , (be not discouraged when those of the Word place obstacles in your path.) After having overcome that, we both laughed and he informed me that he was told there were two paths to the cross, one went further around, was longer, but less steep and maybe easier to climb. It was here I got my second revelation, (Jeremiah had not even tried to get to the cross himself, so he had no personal knowledge of what real obstacles were before me! Many will attempt to deter you from your quest with excuses given them by others!) My reply was that it might be more exhausting going the long way around and thereby take me longer to get to the cross by my wasting my efforts going in an around about way. Jeremiah then pointed me in the direction of the two paths, and I proceeded off on my journey. As I was starting on my way. I felt something in my shoe, my first thought was to ignore it, what could it be, probably just my thoughts. I went a few more steps, again what is that in my shoe, my third encounter with revelation, sit down, take off my shoe and see what the bother was, if nothing is there, be on your way; **sometimes we think we know where the irritation is but won't stop to investigate the answer**. I took off my shoe and behold about 42 cents in change had fallen in my shoe from my pant pocket. The change would have been a hindrance to me on my walk and created a problem for me by way of sore feet which would have lasted longer. My next revelation came when I went too far around starting my ascent. Because I went too far around, I discovered the two trails are nearly next to each other. As I past their intersection I realized I would have saved time taking the path which looked longer. (**if we know the right path in the beginning, we save time**). I began my walk starting out rather nicely; energy is up, purpose set, eye on the goal, all that sort of thing. Not far on my way my legs got tight, my breath gets rapid, and my brow starts to sweat. I look back to see how far I've come, not nearly as far as I have to go (revelation again). I have thoughts of understanding why people turn around after a time on this road, then I see a colony of ants (black ants). These are small creations to teach one a lesson (another revelation). All of them working fast to accomplish Whatever task they have. I then got another revelation of the need to press on in the face of difficulty keeping your eye on the goal. The road was not without

obstacles; rocks, gravel, little
gullies, lots of uneven spots, sometime having to go sideways a
bit to get to a spot where I could continue to go up (another
revelation). May I take this pause to interject, I began to relish
the value of this undertaking more than I could have hoped.
My legs began to get tired, breathing really fast, sweating quite
heavily now. While enjoying my leisurely outing, the remark
about the coyote came to mind, of them maybe causing me
trouble. The thought came to me to pick up as many rocks
as would make me feel comfortable and to continue on
my way. (The Spirit will build you up if you let Him). After
the revelation about the rocks, I began to feel confident
whatever I ran across, I could handle. I had a vision of
taking the coyote by the neck and strangling him, bringing
him back with me after I had made my junket to
the cross. Fear of failure was replaced with zeal of a
ccomplishment! I then noticed a stink bug, a small hindrance,
but it slowed my walk to the cross just long enough to take
notice of it and wonder what problem it might cause me.
About that time I took another look back (too far up to turn
around now), then continued forward towards my goal. I came
upon a place in the walk that, though uphill, really got easy,
and for a short time I felt no strain as I kept pressing forward.
This made me feel exhilarated because I was so close to my goal
**(after struggling for a time there will be those moments when
it gets easier to press toward the goals you set).** While still
dodging rocks, loose gravel, small gullies, and stinkbugs. Moving
shrubbery out of the way, kept going until I came upon those last
few yards. With goal in sight, the uneven ground, the gravel, the
stinkbugs, the fatigue, the coyote, none of that mattered because

I could see the reward. At the cross I fell on my knees because I didn't know how else to express my glee in having made the journey. I looked back over my path and could see where I had come; I could see the smog from where I was which I couldn't see from below. **(We can see the state we're in from a more informed position).** While I sat there looking around enjoying the feeling of accomplishment, I saw two people coming up the trail and they took the best road, were making good time and began to struggle. The thought came to me, "you may be moved to go down to help them but you had to struggle from there to get where you are now. You can tell them how to help themselves by encouraging them to come where you are". I did. They turned around at about half way, just before the easy part came. **On my way down, I noticed how fast one began to go down after struggling so hard to get to an elevated place.** Had I wanted to turn around, the downhill pull would require twice the effort to stop than to continue down! This is a revelation indeed! Enjoy reading the small stories I have prepared for you. Remember it is the seemingly small things in our lives, which will make the most important changes.

Sherman Dickinson

I know what my feelings are

I know what my feelings are
But I don't know
What I'm feeling.
I have a calling on my life,
That my wisdom's not revealing.
I do know how to
Reach my God,
My pride
Won't let me though.
How can I want
The closeness,
And still hide from Him so.
I want to be used of God,
If He'd take the paths I've set.
I don't know why He won't use
The brilliant thoughts I get.
It shouldn't matter
Sometimes I'm wrong,
And that I can't see clearly.
He still should do it my way,
But no I guess not really.
I know what my feelings are,
But I don't know
What I'm feeling,
My senses keep me challenged,
And my soul is
In need of healing.

I have a need, a wanting
To do what's right and yet,
The things I don't want
In my life,
Are things I tend to get.
I know what my feelings are
But I've not felt this before,
It's familiar but different,
But why, I'm just not sure.
I heard the Spirit will show me
What God wants me to do.
If I stop trying to help Him
The vision will come rough.
I know what my feelings are
But I don't know
What I'm feeling.
I find my peace, my comfort,
When at my altar kneeling,
I know what my feelings are,
But I don't know
What I'm feeling,
Is what your self
Will do to you.
Stay in prayer,
Lean not to flesh,
And God will pull you through.

Within the Pages

Within the pages
You find your key,
To open the lock to eternity.
If we know what to expect,
What to look out for,
We won't be so quick,
To be doubtful for sure.
The freewill you have,
Is yours to keep,
When you use it right,
It allows you to sleep.
We want to take credit,
For the things not our doing,
And not for the drama
We keep pursuing.
Within the scriptures,
A lifestyle waits,
A power you'll have
That Satan still hates.
Without knowledge we perish,
This we know,
NO JESUS, NO SAVIOR.
To hell we go.

In the beginning

In the beginning
We never realize
It's not how you
Meet that someone,
But why you meet
That someone,
And don't want to let go.
Something important,
Is not important,
Until it fills something
In you,
That matters.
I have not only
Come to know this,
I am pleased I was not
Ignorant to its
Significance.

I pray to stay open
To you
And your insight.
And I pray God will
Equip me to be
Of one accord with you.
You are a gift
I would like to
Keep and cherish.
May God give me the
Strength to change,
I pray for the
Willingness to change,
That which will enhance
Our relationship,
And the courage to grow
With His instruction.

If I come to be deaf today

If I come to be deaf today
Would my search
For God be over?
If I come to be deaf today
Could I still enjoy a clover?
Could I still touch its petals?
Would it still smell as sweet?
Would I still feel
The earth
He made
Solid beneath my feet.
If I come to be deaf today,
Would I make a new selection?
Would I become bitter then,
Would my prayers
Take new direction?
Would I insert some
New need now,
Or stop and have reflection.
If I come to be deaf today
Could I still be used in spite?
With all that He has done for me,
Would it cancel out my light?

f I come to be deaf today
Would I feel that it's not fair?
Could someone hear God better?
What would He place there?
If I come to be deaf today,
Would I seek God
With my heart?
Might I hear what
He's trying to tell me.
Could this be a new start?
If I come to be deaf today
Would I see a little clearer?
Could He use me better now,
Would I keep His word yet nearer?
If I come to be deaf today,
Will He use me then?
Although I often wonder how,
I really wonder when.
If I come to be deaf today,
I think I understand,
I still could do a work for God,
And preach across the land.

The first step

The first step to growing
Is knowing,
The first step to learning
Is the yearning.
Without the want to advance,
You won't.
Without the motivation
You don't.
Yearning,
Is realizing you
Have to do it
Yourself.
Motivation
Is you
Doing it yourself.

Starting all over

Starting all over!?
Can you do that?
Like plucking a clover.
Can you put the leaves back?
Starting all over
You have to know the way.
But the path changes,
Is different day by day.
To begin again,
You have to go blind,
Forget where you've been,
Take the same road
Another time.
To go back
Is not what you want,
To go on is what you need.
Gather your moments,
Keep your misses,
On your mistakes begin to feed.
The road is clearer
With the map held nearer
And all the pages
Still there to read.

Lives are ruined by...

Lives are ruined by...
Alcohol and by drugs.
Eating too much
As well as by cheating.
Lives are ruined by
Loneliness and
Loving too hard.
Lives are ruined by
Others
By fear.
Lives are ruined by
Choices.
Lives are ruined by
Confidence in
The wrong things.
By ignorance.
Lives are ruined by hating.
Even more by religion.
Lives are ruined by laws.
And certainly by time.
Lives are ruined by...
Choices.

Stand up

Stand up
For the
Right things,
Not what
Sounds good,
Not always what's
Favored,
But what
Matters,
This never changes
But it does
Become
More
Camouflaged.

Love of God

How can we know of an answer
And have the answer out of touch.
How can we say we love
When we hate so much.
That we care and stay out of touch.
It's strange to me, hard to see,
Why we stay so blind.
Everyone needs to know,
But few take time to find.
The love of god is passed to you,
Your acceptance shows
by what you do.
This is where we've failed;
All our life we've hailed,
All the wrong things.
Rings and whatnots,
Going to holy buildings
With wrong thoughts,
Trying to make gods
Out of human beings.
Reasons you're chasing,
Looking in wrong places,
Ever wondering why.
The love of god is passed to you,
Your acceptance shows by
what you do.

What do you do then?

It's easy to pass
When there's no test.
Easy to look good
When it's not our best.
We can all handle it,
When there's no stress.
But what if,
What when,
You have to fight for it,
What do you do then?
What do you say?
What do you feel?
When the struggles
Are No longer thoughts,
When the Threat
Becomes real!
What do you do then?
How do you recover,
Rediscover,
All that was good
For you then.

Where do you go,
At the end of the show?
When the play
Becomes real.
When it's no longer
An act,
And you begin to feel.
What do you do then?
When your rock
Starts to reel,
When the cute,
Has no appeal,
The one you
Want to know,
Will begin to show,
And their heart
To you they'll lend,
You may not agree,
With all that you see,
It you look
You find a friend.
If you find that you,
Can be one too,
What do you do then?

Why does it have to be that way

Ever try to explain yourself
And really not know why?
Wonder why you should
Commit yourself
Until the day you die.
That's what love is
Wrapped up in compassion,
It makes you put your
Soul out there,
While your feeling
Take a bashing.
Why does it have to be
That way?
Ever say you won't
Do that again
Because you're smarter now
Got sucked right back any-
way,
And didn't really know how.
I tell you the more I study
The more I confuse myself.
Things I put away,
Keep getting off the shelf.
Why does it have to be
That way?

Ever wonder why
What you want
Evades you with all vigor.
No matter what
The price You pay,
It's really a small figure.
Ever tried to find
What love was,
And found what it
Was not .Attempt to hold ,
your sanity, with all
the strength you've got.
Of all the things
We're blessed to get,
Whether given or we
Buy it, don't doubt the
Worth of having love,
At least until you try it.

I've been hurt too

I think of the Hurt
I've done to you,
And reflect on the fact
I've been hurt too.
If there's someone
you want,
But just can't get,
You find others to be with,
And yet,
It's not the same.
You enjoy the time,
The moments seem prime,
Their emotions you
Proceed To maim.
Why is that?
I've been hurt too.
You try to tease,
Begin to squeeze
Them into the mold you
miss. Why do we do,
Can't help but go through,
Such foolishness as this.
All you want to do,
Cause I've been hurt too,
Is examine that someone close,
To find one real,
That you can love,
Is what you want the most.

I Love what you do

Once we learn to praise
What's there and not
What's lacking ,
We can love as we should
And stop acting.
Just cause you don't curse,
A fact most pleasing,
Should not fuel
My love for you.
It's not the things
I hope you aren't
But it's certainly
The things you do.
Do not give time
To things You hate,
It's hard to believe,
But we grow what
We Cultivate.

We spend time on
What we want to,
Who cares what you say
I love what you do.
You don't want to lose
What's yours.
Realize too little too late,
Reaching for the latch,
With the prize out the gate.
I love what you do,
Could be said more often
And while they can hear it
Not when in a coffin.

Freedom you desire
Easy life.
Things and strife,
Searched for without
cease,
We've time for wine,
Time for lying,
But no time for peace.
Warm up your heart,
Create a spark,
In *someone else's* life.
Use your mind
For good this time,
And sleep for once
Tonight.
You attain,
You desire,
You desire,
You desire.

False Gods

I don't worship
False gods
As you can plainly see,
Could not imagine
Being taken by such
Weak security.
My education won't let me
Fall for that,
I won't be sucked in,
My pockets are too fat.
People love
to see me coming
Because of the power I yield.
Many skylines are graced
By the structures I build.
I don't have time
For false gods,
I've got too much to do.
I'm not setting around idle,
Worshipping some
Statue like you.
People need what I have
And the things that
I give them.

I love seeing people
Who dance to my rhythm.
I've heard people worship
gods they don't know of,
Some even worship
Some God up above.
I love showing
What I've done,
With my wall full of
Plaques, why spend time
On Jesus or something
As worthless as that.
Don't have much peace,
Have to watch what I got,
Some people are trusting,
I'm glad that I'm not.
Got to set some new goals,
Don't want to be lacking,

**Those things that
Are our gods,**
Are the things
We keep tracking.

What If

What if
You are the one,
And I act like I can't see it.
What if
You want that someone
And I pretend I can't be it.
What if
My choice, my chance,
Came down to this.
You get many moments,
But this one
You can't miss.
What if
All of what you
Have gone through,
Could pale
By this experience,
Suddenly what you've endured,
Has no relevance.
How would you know,
If you don't put
Your full self into it.

Because if this is the one,
It is the only way to do it.
We wax eloquent
On the one
That got away,
Those missed experiences
Prepared you for this day.
While it is true,
We cannot know
How things will turn out.
What if
This is the one
You had been
Dreaming about.

Actions speak louder than words

If you look closely,
Or even if you won't,
You know someone cares,
And when they don't.
Actions speak louder
than words.
We all know those
Who speak one way,
And act another,
Say they will be there for you
Just like a brother.
Ezra was my Uncle,
I'm blessed by that fact,
You know how he treated you,
Wasn't an act.
You can tell someone cares
By the way they treat you,
If you need them to help,
They try to come through.
Ezra was like that,
He had a tough cover,
And a heart which was fat.
Actions speak louder
than words.
What makes a good father,
Husband or friend?
An ear to listen,
And compassion
Without end.
Of the deeds he did,
He didn't boast much.
Give some money,
Lend a hand,
Free advice and such.
He had a way he smiled
When he fussed at you,
Raise his voice,
Puff up his Lips,
Would punch you too.
I've finished my story
And one thought
Comes through,
His actions spoke louder
Than words.
How about you?

A young girl sits dreamless

A young girl sits dreamless
Is only inspired by vision Seem less.
So much of what was----gone,
Of what's to be----vague.
So much of what she had----Broken,
Of what was,
Remain mere tokens.
A young girl sits dreamless
Is only inspired by seeking,
For the things in her past,
Which are still worth keeping.
A young girl sits dreamless
Will still possess a need,
Have good thoughts,
And a will to succeed.
Is only inspired by love,
From someone who's thought
What she is thinking of.

A young girl sits dreamless
Has no cause to fret,
There are other pleasures
And new dreams to get.
A young girl sits
Dreamless,
Is only inspired by success.
Not what she has,
What she didn't get.
Not what she found,
What she hasn't
Found yet.
She will have it,
Is a good bet.
A young girl sits
Dreamless,
Is inspired by
her character,
Encouraged by integrity.
For all that matters,
This matters
most you see.

I'm pointing no fingers

I have been there
And my memory Ain't hazy.
I'm pointing no fingers,
But I'm boasting like crazy.
I had time
To clean up the mess
Realize I've been blessed,
And turn my life around.
Spread the joy, the happiness,
For the new path I've found.
It's not too late,
No matter the date,
To change the path you're on.
God gave the key,
The answer you see,
When He gave us
His only Son.

I'm pointing no fingers,
'Cause I realize you flee.
I was someone else.
Nowhere near
Who I'm growing to be.
I take my knocks,
The choices I've made,
Tell someone else,
Or the answer will fade.
I'm pointing no fingers
'Cause of what I went
Through, I'm going to
Help someone,
And you can too.

What do I want

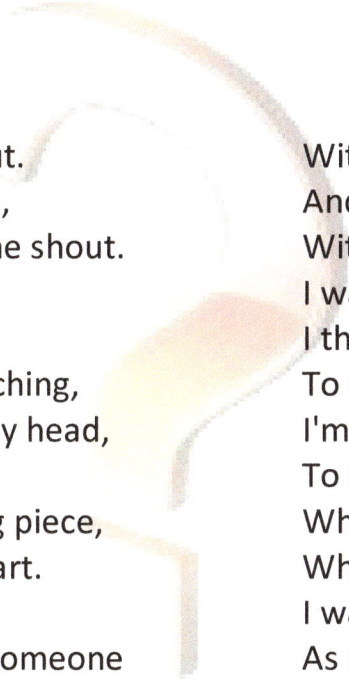

What do I want?
I want someone
Like you,
From the inside out.
I want compassion,
Enough to make me shout.
I want to be there
For someone.
Want to stop searching,
For that thing in my head,
In my heart.
I need that missing piece,
Need that other part.
What do I want?
I want to be with someone
Long enough,
To find out who they are,
And what's locked deep
In their heart.
I want to feel safe

With you,
And feel, you feel safe
With me too.
I want to smile when
I think of you,
To feel empty when
I'm away from you,
To feel warm
When I hold you.
What do I want?
I want you to love me,
As much as I love you.
What do I want?
I want this dream
To never end...

Depend on him

Is it testimonies or
Blessings,
What we go through?
It depends
On the outcome,
And the spirit in you.
If He's inside,
As you confess,
You know at
Your worst,
He's at His best.
If "Thank-you-Lord,"
Is what you profess,
Then depend on Him,
To release your stress.
To continue to struggle
With what you
Can't change,
Means you have
No faith
To release the reins.
Easier said than done,
That's for sure,
But scripture and prayer
Will help the cure.

I can't love you if I don't know you

I can't love you
If I don't know you.
Can't make love to you,
If you won't show me
Where you are.
My need to be there for you,
Can only take me so far.
I can't touch those places
Dear to you,
Those hurts
Near to you,
How can I heal
Your pain,
If I can't see it.
Why do you make me beg;
To know you,
To get close to you,
To be part of you.
I can't love you,
If I don't know you,
And your walls are
Too high to climb.

I need a door,
That's for sure,
And you have the key.
If you let me in,
I'll be a friend,
And a comfort to some degree.
Show me that part
Locked deep in your heart.
I'll prescribe the remedy.
There's no way you can feel,
A love that's real,
If you won't allow me to see.
Put our backs into it,
Put your trust all through it,
Oh! How strong
Four shoulders can be.
I can't love you
If I don't know you,
And I would like to, you see.

Lives are ruined by...

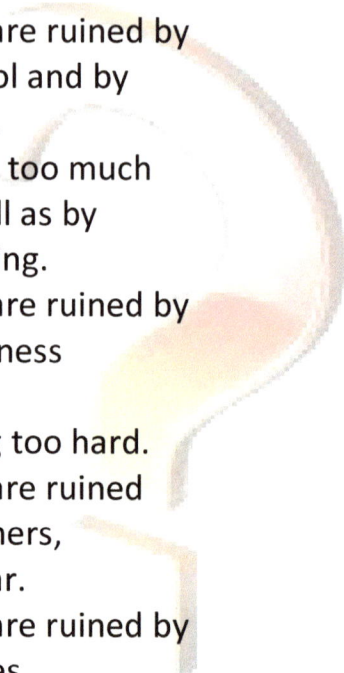

Lives are ruined by
Alcohol and by
Drugs.
Eating too much
As well as by
Cheating.
Lives are ruined by
Loneliness
And
Loving too hard.
Lives are ruined
By Others,
By Fear.
Lives are ruined by
Choices.
Lives are ruined by
Confidence in
The wrong things.
By ignorance.
Lives are ruined by
Hating.
Even more by
Religion.
Lives are ruined by
Laws.
And certainly by
Time.
Lives are ruined by
                    Choices.

A Declaration

I have studied the properties of death,
Foreseen my fai1ure
Long enough.
It's time to advance myself,
Dare to be happy
For once.
Make some things go down;
Tired of being affected by chance.
1t's the way you,
Not where you,
Spend your thoughts.
Buying time is fantasy.
What you have
Is all you have
You see.
Use that,
It's all you really need.

Memories worth Keeping

I won't let my past
control my now,
My future,
My what, my when,
My how.
I won't make you pay,
In anyway,
For someone else today.
Won't stop my next move,
'Cause I've nothing to prove,
My life will be as I make it.
My task for now,
Be happy, and how,
To feel it, and not fake it.
I will take my issues,
My recent stumbles,
Grasp my pain,
And my senses jumbled.
Take note of those right results,
Cast off those visions,
Which make me sulk,
Hold on to what's fleeting;
A good relationship,
And memories worth keeping.

Purpose

When I am faced
With a choice,
It is my purpose that
Motivates me.
That is important to understand.
What am I trying to do?
Be purposeful in your pursuits.
A positive endeavor failed,
Is more fruitful,
Than an evil intent accomplished.
We have a responsibility
To the spiritual well being
Of each other.
What drives us?
What do we wish we had?
Nothing is more powerful
Than purpose.
It justifies too many things.
It grows so much stuff.
Ego feeds on purpose.
Self needs purpose.
The spirit only needs peace.
The flesh drives our purpose.
This we can't change.
But we can direct
It's energies.
Purpose.

It's okay to be scared

It's okay to be scared
But you won't grow
Till you've shared,
The love that's in your heart.
What you have to give,
A full life to live,
You won't know until you start.
You just don't know,
How far you can go.
And you're afraid of injury.
What you have to unfold,
Makes it hard to hold,
The peace that for you could be.
It's okay to be scared,
But you won't live
Till you've dared
To love someone, you see.
You must release,
To enjoy that peace,
Of someone close to you,
Cause trials will come
And you'll need someone
To help to pull you through.

Death is no stranger

Death is no villain
It does not take in spite.
It's your deeds,
Your actions,
That keeps you up
At night.
Death is no stranger,
We see it night and day,
Why pretend
We don't know it,
Never experienced
Its saddening way.
Death is no stranger
It knows who
You and I are.
Maybe not at your Doorstep,
But certainly not too far.
Got to get a new dress,
Got to have a new car.
Got to get your mind right
Before you go too far.
Death is no stranger,
Just you wait and see,
When you get a visit
No matter where you be.

Because of

Because of
The way I feel about you
When I don't want to.
The decisions I make
When I don't have to.
Those things I've enjoyed
With you,
And those I hope to,
I know I love you.
Because of the difference
You've made
Since I've met you.
The memories of
Times together
I pursue.
Those feelings
So freely shown.
Because of
My comparing others
To you.
And feeling so clearly blessed.
I take little credit
For your sorting
Me out from all the rest.

Emotional treasures

I have an
Emotional treasure chest.
And my treasures are heavy.
I've tried to throw them
Away...
I think.
Thought of starting
A new treasure hunt,
But the thought
Weakens me.
All the moments
Placed therein,
Can't be emptied.
Not by carelessness,
Or vicious intent.
And it is hard
To build
A lifetime
Again.

Artist

Artist.
A person
Wanting
To show you
Something,
A thing,
They think is beautiful,
On some level.
We must all
Be artists.
Being able
To express.
Education through
Entertainment.
Because it holds
Your attention.
Often times before
It holds your
Interest.
Artist.
Yeah.

Time passes so quickly

Time Passes so quickly.
Before you know it,
Your looks have changed.
People you love have died.
Your children are all grown up.
Your life's expenditure is met.
And you are on the next road.
Who knows what they will get?
There are those few,
Those peaceful,
Those saved who believe,
Have confidence that,
Are encouraged by,
Relieved,
They know what is next.
We can't know
The future,
For everyone,
(we would mess it up).
But we can have a confidence
Because of what God
Is continually doing.
And...
When you watch
God work,
Time passes so quickly.

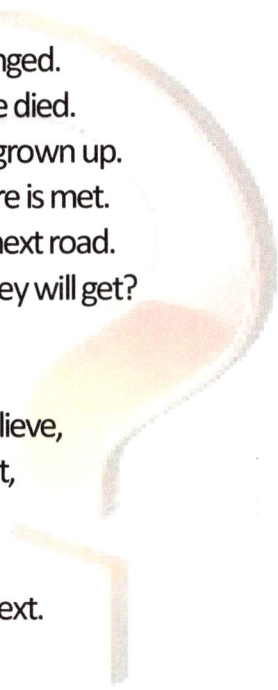

Your parent

Thought you knew something
About your parents.
We know they reach
To get something
From us.
Teaching a part,
Touching a part,
Tearing apart.
They have the advantage,
They spend
Their adult life
Watching you,
Probing you,
Guiding you.
As you mature
And you begin
To learn.
Just before
You drain
Their brain,
It's time to
Make your way.
They won't share
How they got there,
And you will
Be that
One day.

Been there all the time

I tried other stuff.
Got satisfaction
From the information,
But there was still That lack,
That something, that peace,
I was missing.
You see,
I know I am seeking
Peace.
Not happiness,
Not recognition, not power,...
Peace.
That peace which escapes
My reason,
That I know is there,
But I don't know how it got in.
I know a place.
Having the knowledge
You need.
It does require you read.
Found in a book.
Oh, how we do enjoy
Our books,
This one is so fulfilling,
I can't put it down...
The bible,
Been there all the time.

You were made for me
You're a manifestation
Of my imagination,
You were made for me.
I thank the Lord,
'Cause from my heart
He created you.
From the top
Of your head.
To the tip of your toe,
You're compassion
Through and through.
With Jesus as my guide,
I'm made perfect inside
With love as my covering
I have God by my side,
And you in my stride,
I feel like I'm hovering.
Everything I'm missing
You've got,
All the fears I've had,
You're not.
When I become insecure,
Of the next day unsure,
You're there for me,
One, two, three.
When I'm in your arms
And a slave to your charms,
I'm happy as can be.
God knows what we need,
Yes, of this I've decreed,
You were made for me.

Truly a gift

I'm intrigued
While perplexed
At the same time.
You are truly a gift,
A precious find.
The effort to focus,
And make it all fit,
To try to feel worthy
Of what I'm
Blessed with.
You show much courage
But you're vulnerable too,
Have no problem loving,
It's will they love you.
To be part of a world
So warped and confused,
To want to be kind
And not to be used.
There's so much of you
That you want to share,
The only task left is,
Whom you'll place there.

In our life we're tested
With change and choices,
And we try to respond
To the right voices.
Don't want to be miffed
By what we go through,
You are truly a gift,
And I'm someone
Who loves you.

Your face

Just in case
I can't say it later.
I say thank You Lord,
For allowing me the memories.
The lessons I did learn.
The genuine people
I did meet.
Thank You Lord,
For those scary moments,
They bring me back to You.
To reality. To my need
To stay close,
To You Lord.
Thank You Lord.
For all that You have
Done for me.
Thank You for my family,
For my peace.
For my relationship
With You.
For the tolerance
Shown in the inner peace
You let me keep.
I want so to show others
Your face.

On so many levels

On so many levels,
He who is
Better at it,
Gets better
Rewarded for it.
To be blessed
With that,
To be rewarded
For that,
To be burdened
With that,
On so many levels
Requires,
Demands,
A direction
Better than our own.
We must be
Wise enough
To listen.
To everything.
God gives lessons
On so many levels.

It still works

It still works.
That is what's important
You know.
If you have benefitted
A day or a decade,
It still works.
It still does what
You hoped
It would do.
Today.
That is beautiful.
And should be
Appreciated.
Especially if
There are a lot
Of days attached.
Prayer.
It still works.

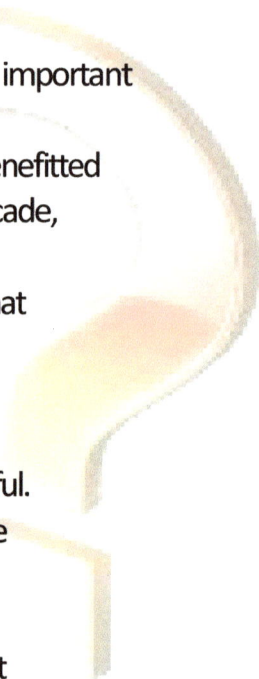

No matter what

'No matter what'
Sure rolls off
The tongue
Easily enough.
On the surface
It makes one stick
Their chest out
On it's verbiage
But the truth
Is arduous
And we grow
To appreciate
It's weight.

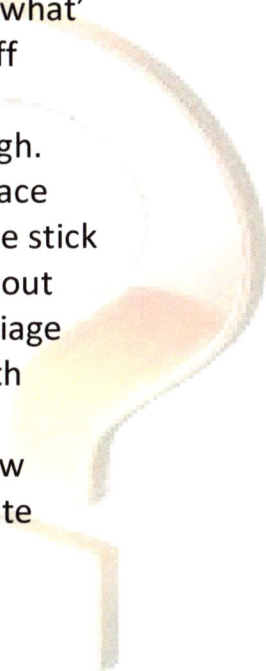

This visit

Thank You Lord.
Thank You for what I think
I feel I'm feeling.
Thank You for putting
A part inside
I don't control,
Which allows me contact
With you.
Thank You Lord
For confusions past.
It showed me
Your hand.
Thank You for the moments
I can't explain.
It makes me BELIEVE
You are real.
I know the struggle
Is with me.
Thank You Lord,
For Your hand through this.
Thank You for the growth.
Thank You for the protection,
And the times
You let me see You work.
Small things,
But real things.
Thank You for now Lord.
I have really enjoyed
This visit.

How do you feel?

How do you feel
When there is that
Seeking...
Some imbibe.
And the container
Is where it
Should be,
But the contents
Are not,
Man, that just
Does something
To me.

Nothing To Lose

Nothing to lose,
But something to forget,
The thing which was
Holding you back.
Is it clear what you're
Holding on to and why?
When this very activity
Has you dreading
What you get
When you die.
You would think,
You would be happy,
Knowing you will reach
What you strive for;
Perfection, eternity,
Trying to get it while
You sleep.
Cannot reach what
You run from
Bad seed you were breached.
The past that you hide from,
Was intended to teach
You how much we need each other.

The rules have not changed,
It is you being foolish
Enough to feel your
Input matters
Not what you think
Of how things should be run
Into that wall
Again and again.
Wanting to make changes
And start a new trend.
The more you deny
your purpose,
The more lost you get
To use your will
You begin to take
This serious.
Your need to be free
Just makes God furious.

The prize

If you don't care
It doesn't matter,
Then it's easy.
But, if you do care,
You can't stop it.
You feel it.
Yea, it's work.
You either get
The prize,
Or you don't.
Prize.
Same feeling
As gift,
But you put in all
The work.

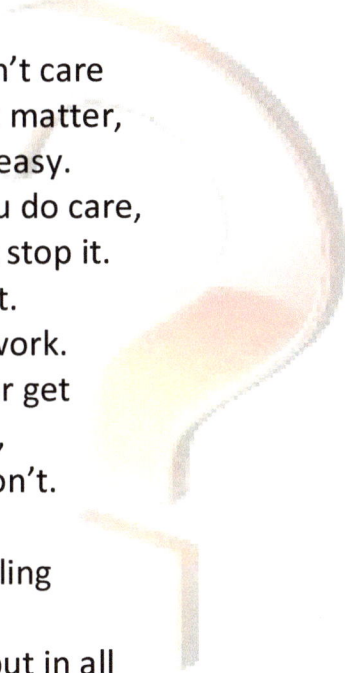

You seek it

You are able to
Appreciate
Being in love
On a more
Significant level.
You seek it.
For the right reasons.
You understand
The treasures
To be uncovered
With someone
Who loves as deeply
As you do.
You seek it.
You are changed
By its anticipation.
Rejuvenated by
It's strengths.
That is our secret,
Two people
In love,
Are so much stronger.
You seek it.

Things I call relaxing

I want to do things
I call relaxing.
I don't need more stuff.
It changes nothing,
Creates only fluff.
I want the one
Close to me,
Just to be
Trustworthy.
Receiving my love
sincerely.
Reviewing our victories
 dearly.
I know the process...
Oh, less I digress...
I want to do things
I call relaxing.
It used to be fun,
Chasing that stress,
Scrambling, recovering
From all kinds of mess.
That moves me
No more.

The nonsensical risks,
The Ego trips.
Business that is brisk,
And the tax rips.
I want to do things
I call relaxing.
To fight the good fight,
Even if you have one,
Is not something to
pursue.
Relaxing...
Is the thing to do.
To chase, to grow
To a place we left,
Usually when we
Close to death.
To a place we had,
While dragging more
clutter.
Trying to steer
With a broken rudder...
I want to do things
I call relaxing.

Wasting time?

Don't waste another day,
Heard that a hundred time
A dozen ways.
What is wasting time?
Writing rhyme,
Watching planes flying,
Shooting people
And watch them dying.
What is wasting time?
Who's to say,
You should
Waste time their way.
Who's to steer you
In the useful direction?
You know what you want,
Or should,
And what end results will be.
Wasting time,
Looks like thinking to me.

We don't believe it

People must begin.
We don't believe it.
We reason, at most,
Our struggle with
Each other.
And of that we boast.
If we knew it
We would stop,
And that's not the case.
To know, we believe,
What's clear in our face.
People are dying.
Do we know it?
Our life style,
Is trying,
Will we stow it?
Bling, bling,
Rather than
Offspring.
What matters
Centers around us.
It's all we see, all we trust.
Can't enjoy what we own,
Moments being squeezed
Into other time zones.
We have enough
To struggle to keep.
Loan interest mounting
As we sleep.
The office,
Our real home,
where we always
seem to be.
If we can't come
together,
How can we be free.
Personal wins
Is not success,
We must unite
With all the rest.
We don't believe it.
Brainwashed, not lit.
Someone has to start,
Someone has to quit...
Clearly, so clearly...
We don't believe it.

Have you ever wondered

Have you ever wondered,
Why you wanted something
So bad,
You would risk,
Or wanted to?
Got this nagging desire,
This itch that bothered you.
Have you ever
Wanted something
So long, it felt like a need,
Thought how much
You'd be willing to lose,
And not to retrieve.
Have you ever thought,
Maybe you were chasing
Too hard,
Getting careless,
Overlooking some important fact,
Not applying some test.
Have you ever spent more time
Wondering, if you deserve it,
Than if you could handle it.
Looked at what you liked,
And ignored the rest.

Ever felt something tugging
Some tightening in your chest.
Felt by now you had a knack.
thought it was pulling you on
And it was pulling you back.
Have you ever
Heard something troubling
About the thing you envision,
Didn't give it much thought
Cause people will bring
Division.
Have you ever
Accepted something
You really can't tolerate.
Ever wondered why
Relationships fail,
When they're no longer
A date.
Have you ever wondered
Why we ignore a clue.
I know you've wondered,
I've wondered too.

Looking for one

I'm looking for one.
But,
For those wanting
To play,
Let the games begin.
They would need
To know the game
Anyway.
You have to know why
Before you know what.
I would have it
No other way.
It would,
After all,
Have to be
Different.

I Will Celebrate Differently

I will celebrate differently
This holiday season,
My thanks will go deeper
Than Christ is the reason.
Our focus should never
Have been gift giving,
Lately I thought of the
Blessing of living.
I will celebrate differently
This holiday season,
I hope to do something
For Christ that's pleasing.
Our days are so short,
This life is so fleeting.
Our minds should prepare
For our God we'll be meeting.
Let's take time to be thankful
For what we've been
Blessed with,
Try not to hope for
What presents we'll get.
There are families which
Have nothing,
No presents, no tree.
Why then does God keep blessing
Someone like me?
I will celebrate differently
This holiday season.

Give thanks for my home
Under warm covers I'm easing.
Christmas is not about
Gifts and such,
It's to remind us that
God loves us so much.
Let's try to talk less,
And do something today,
Help show someone else
That Christ is the way.

Right now

Right now,
I have not
Offended you,
You have not said
That which would
Make me
Retaliate.
Right now,
We have…
No reason
To be angry.
Right now
We can…
Determine
What we will…
Grow.
Right now
Is all we have
Between us.
Be more
Intent on
Positive use
Of our…
Right now.

Why

Why,
Has to make sense.
Really make sense.
Or it drains you.
Sacrifice is fine,
Commendable.
But it's that
Why,
What part of us
Has been nurtured,
Developed,
Depended on,
To fuel our----
Why.
Moralistic?
No longer
An issue.
Ah, but there
Is still - you.
Your vanity,
Maybe your
Selfishness.
Allowed to
Run amok.
Why!

I Want To Be In Love

I want to be in love,
I just don't want it now.
Want to feel its comfort,
I just do not know how.
I want to have its strengths
Without its weaknesses.
Want to be its participant,
Instead of just its witness.
I want to feel
The peace it has,
But not the pain it brings.
Want to stay in control
And not begin to cling.
I want to be in love,
With someone
To show me how.
I want to feel the closeness
I'm just not ready now.
I want someone to smile
When they hear my name,
To rush home to someone
I miss,

And hope they feel the same.
I want to be the warmth inside
Someone's heart and spirit.
I know how to say I love,
But there's no one to hear it.
I want to be in love
Because I miss it so.
Want to hold that someone
Close,
Will God bless me though?
I want to see myself
In their eyes,
While I clear their face
From mine.
I want to share my everything
With them,
Until I'm out of time.
I want to be in love again,
Because nothing else is like it.
I have seen them come,
I have seen them go,
Where is the love
That I get?

Open our eyes

Let's stop fooling ourselves,
  Open ourselves
To reality.
This present form   Love got you here,
Of which we're encased, Can help you here,
Being a means   And bring you God near.
Has an end,   Jesus, having been
Which is waste.   Through it,
Jesus wants you to be Can help you do it,
Happy through eternity. With rewards
He is coming and   You can't realize.
Every eye will see.   Do as you will with your time,
Open our eyes,   And all that will materialize.
No one knows what   Take time to see,
Tomorrow may bring.   Jesus wants you to be,
Why spend our now,   Happy for eternity,
Our mind,   He is coming,
On hate, revenge   And every eye
And things of that kind, Will see, will see.

I want to be a witness

I want to be a witness
But I struggle with
My condition.
I feel there is something
I don't have yet,
That I'm still in
A transition.
I don't know if
I could tell someone,
Or rather if they'd
Believe me.
How can I be
A light somewhere
It took so long to see.
I want to be a witness,
Not do more harm than good.
God don't have to talk to me
But I still pray that he would.
You know I think I've heard Him,
Alas, and didn't know it.
Lost what He left for me to use,
'Cause I didn't know
Where I stowed it.

I tell you this
Don't be remiss
It's me holding me back.
God will use me,
Heal me, bless me,
If I just get on the track.
I have this urge,
This yearning,
Of what I should
Say to you.
Unfold your arms,
Reach out your heart
And you will be used too.

So You're In Love

So you're in love?
Are you lonely?
Love won't fix that.
Need someone to Keep
You warm at night?
Love won't fix that.
You want someone
To talk to
When the sun
Is just right?
Hold you close in the
Soft moonlight.
Love won't fix that.
You need a person,
And that's a fact.
And that person
Has to love you back.
Sometimes love gets
The blame though,
Keeping you there
While the others go.
What do you hope to get?
Have you gotten enough
Bruises yet?
Are you far enough in
To not want to
Come out?
So you're in love?
Somehow I doubt.

How do you know?
You won't be sure
For a year or so.
The words passed
May be prickly,
And the deeds
Will certainly
Mount up
Quickly.
Love is no mystery.
There are only two kinds,
The way it affects you,
Either pull or binds.
So your actions
Must be weighted
Thoughtfully.
You need someone
To love you truthfully.
Love strengthens
But weakens.
Bonds but separates.
You will be surprised
How much courage
It takes.
Can you be in that?
Do you want to try?
One thing is certain,
No wimps, no wimps
Need apply.

Mystery of emotion

The mystery of emotion
Together with its power,
Is as stimulating
And refreshing
As a cool, cool shower.
The need, for those
That have it, Is real,
The desire to
Express it is deep,
Sometimes escaping,
When you rather
It would keep.
The weakness you feel,
Taken over by its suggestions,
Can make you feel helpless,
A slave to its possession.
But the joy that you feel
Along with the pride,
Can make you put worry,
And walls aside.
The gift to give it,
To lighten someone's load
Is reward enough,

And sometimes twofold,
To give is to get,
Without question is true,
To be blinded
By its magic
Is a reality to.
The rush you feel,
The peace you gather,
To love someone
Is a serious matter,
You can't control it,
Just keep it at bay.
You try to contain it,
Just keep it at bay.
You try to contain it,
It escapes anyway,
Each scar is deeper,
Each memory more lasting,
Why can't we stop feeling it,
A question worth asking,
Cause sometimes it works,
And it lasts too,
If you're given love
As well as you do.

Why children

Why children?
Because they are windows.
They are sponges.
They are recorders,
They are mimics,
They are unpredictable,
They are honest,
At first.
They are sweet,
At birth.
They are remedies
They are deterrents,
They are loyal,
They are forgiving,
Or so they say, anyway.
They are clones. they are gifts,
They are blessings.
They are hard to believe.
They are energetic.
They are filters, they are shields,
They are your conscience.
They are your gauges,
They are date testers,
They are money ciphers
,
      They are you.

What can you do?

Have you ever been troubled?
Troubled about yourself.
Trying to best use your time,
What little you may have left.
Finding your direction lost,
Your attention scattered,
Good intentions disappear
As if they didn't matter.
What can you do?
Brothers, sisters, and families part,
Everyone wanting to love,
No one wanting to start.
What can you do?
Turn to God,
Reach Him through prayer,
You'll find comfort, strength,
Love waiting there.
God knows what you are inside.
Find Him, know Him,
Cast off your blinding pride.
To care about life,
Rather its condition
Is best displayed
Through actions
Not wishing.
What can you do?

God is waiting

Why try to hide,
And not know where,
Keep something inside,
The Spirit placed there,
Why have a light
And then sit on it.
And complain about things
That aren't as you want it.
Why struggle to keep
The Spirit at bay
When in due season,
It escapes anyway.
Why hide what God
Has done for you
When what you know,
Can pull others through?
We want to be Christ-like,
Striving to be pure.
This is not the test,
Not the trial to endure.
God would not call us
To something we can't meet,
To do what He tells us,
Is the grander feat.

He calls us to be separate,
To try to do better,
To take what we've learned,
And bring others together.
We can lead by example,
But this we ignore,
This may bring on
A change,
And this we abhor.
God is waiting for you
To come 'round
To pick up your gift,
And the peace
 Which abounds.
Oh, a gift is free,
You cannot work for it.
No matter how you try,
You will not deserve it.
 This is what Christ
Is saying to you,
Bless someone that doesn't
deserve it, too.

Before

How much do you
Have to hurt,
Feel familiar dismay,
Before you reach
For something else,
And try to bridge
Your way.
As we struggle
With ourselves,
Are let down
Once again,
Look up and pray,
This very day,
And ask God to amend.
How much pain
Will it take,
Before you reach
That bend?
Do you need to be
Brought low,
Before you seek a friend?
How much despair

Will you endure,
Before you seek
Some answer.
If where you are
Leaves you unsure,
It's time to cure.
The cancer. You had
better pay attention,
The signs are all there.
You can wait
If you want to,
But you're heading
For a snare.
Don't get too deep,
Or fall asleep,
Don't let your head
Go under,
Save what you have,
It's in your hands,
Before it's torn asunder.
Before we change,
We must first want to
When you begin
Is up to you.

That is where the inside's start

Why so much suffering
Why so much silence.
Why so much selfishness.
Words are cheap,
Easy to get,
To use.
Didn't even waste those.
For the most part.
Any action takes effort.
And some part of
Your heart.
That's why they are
More valuable,
That is where the insides start.

\

In spite of all the light

I sit here and the world
Breaks down in front of me.
Puzzled, amazed that others
Seem not to see.
I find myself involved
In others
Fantasies, tragedies
And frights
Wondering why others
Can't see the madness,
In spite of all the light.
We want to have,
But don't want to work.
To be loved, but not
Give love in return.
It's easy, so easy
Why do we have to take turns,
And let someone else
Love first.
I sit here, and the world
Breaks down in front of me.
I'm subjected, rejected
And involved

Almost in the same degree.
We say we want peace,
Yet we continue to fight,
Why can't we see the madness,
In spite of all the light?
Can it go on like this?
Wishing to be of help
With this love thing
Everyone seems to resist.
Wanting to gather myself,
Climb out of this abyss,
Clinching my mind this time,
Instead of my fist.
We want to have,
But don't want to work,
To be loved but not
Give love in return.
It's easy, so easy,
 Why do we have to take turns,
And let someone else
 Love first.

I know what my feelings are

I know what my feelings are
But I don't know
What I'm feeling.
I have a calling on my life,
That my wisdom's not revealing.
I do know how to
Reach my God,
My pride
Won't let me though.
How can I want
The closeness,
And still hide from Him so.
I want to be used of God,
If He'd take the paths I've set.
I don't know why He won't use
The brilliant thoughts I get.
It shouldn't matter
Sometimes I'm wrong,
And that I can't see clearly.
He still should do it my way,
But no I guess not really.
I know what my feelings are,
But I don't know
What I'm feeling
My senses keep me challenged,
And my soul is
In need of healing.

I have a need, a wanting
To do what's right and yet
The things I don't want
In my life,
Are things I tend to get.
I know what my feelings are
But I've not felt this before,
It's familiar but different,
But why, I'm just not sure.
I heard the Spirit will show me
What God wants me to do.
If I stop trying to help Him
The vision will come through.
I know what my feelings are
But I don't know
What I'm feeling.
I find my peace, my comfort,
When at my altar kneeling,
I know what my feelings are,
But I don't know
What I'm feeling,
Is what your self
Will do to you.
Stay in prayer,
ean not to flesh,
And God will pull you through.

A mate a lover a friend

Let's discuss,
The ultimate rush,
A mate, a lover, a friend.
Someone there for you,
To help pull you through.
When the thick becomes thin.
When the looks reach their end.
When it's dark
Around the bend.
No matter what you do,
They still love you.
Someone you can support
Without fear or retort.
When you have that bout,
They won't walk out,
And you'll be in their arms again.
You see in them now,
What you saw in them then,
A mate, a lover, a friend.
Build your hopes,
Your anticipation,
On the right stuff,
The right compilation.

If God be in it,
There is no limit,
His gifts are divine.
Someone there for you,
To help pull you through,
And give you
Their strength
Each time.

www.ingramcontent.com/pod-product-compliance
Lightning Source LLC
Chambersburg PA
CBHW041529090426
42738CB00035B/10